DATE DUE			

333.8
GOR

C1

3 24571 0900739 7
Gorman, Jacqueline
Laks.

Fossil fuels

What If We Do NOTHING?

FOSSIL FUELS

Jacqueline Laks Gorman

Gareth Stevens
Publishing

Please visit our web site at: www.garethstevens.com.
For a free color catalog describing Gareth Stevens Publishing's list of high-quality books, call 1-800-542-2595 (USA)
or 1-800-387-3178 (Canada). Gareth Stevens Publishing's fax: 1-877-542-2596

Library of Congress Cataloging-in-Publication Data

Gorman, Jacqueline Laks, 1955-
    Fossil fuels / by Jacqueline Laks Gorman.
      p. cm. – (What if we do nothing?)
    Includes bibliographical references and index.
    ISBN-10: 1-4339-0087-4   ISBN-13: 978-1-4339-0087-7 (lib. bdg.)
    1. Fossil fuels. 2. Fossil fuels–Environmental aspects. I. Title.
    TP318.G626   2008
    333.8'2–dc22   2008029214

This North American edition published in 2009 by Gareth Stevens Publishing under license from Arcturus Publishing Limited.
Gareth Stevens Publishing
A Weekly Reader® Company
1 Reader's Digest Road
Pleasantville, NY 10570-7000 USA

Copyright © 2009 by Arcturus Publishing Limited
Produced by Arcturus Publishing Limited
26/27 Bickels Yard, 151-153 Bermondsey Street, London SE1 3HA

Series concept: Alex Woolf
Editor: Alex Woolf
Designer: Phipps Design
Picture researcher: Alex Woolf

Gareth Stevens Managing Editor: Lisa M. Herrington
Gareth Stevens Editor: Jayne Keedle
Gareth Stevens Creative Director: Lisa Donovan

Picture Credits: Corbis: 9 (Colin Keates), 10 (Craig Aurness), 12 (George Steinmetz), 15 (Frederic Larson/*San Francisco Chronicle*), 18 (Remi Benali), 19 (Lara Solt/*Dallas Morning News*), 21 (Narendra Shrestha/EPA), 23 (Fatih Saribas/Reuters), 24 (Reuters), 25 (Will and Deni McIntyre), 28 (Abir Abdullah/EPA), 29 (Tom Bean), 31 (Bjorn Sigurdson/EPA), 32 (*China Daily*/Reuters), 33 (Tom Pietrasik), 36 (Floris Leeuwenberg), 37 (Dane Andrew/ZUMA), 38 (Car Culture), 39 (Dane Andrew/ZUMA), 44 (Roger Ressmeyer). Getty Images: 16, 34 (AFP). Science Photo Library: 6 (Christian Jegou Publiphoto Diffusion), 26 (Gary Hincks), 30 (NASA), 43 (Mark Sykes). Shutterstock: Cover bottom left (Ingvar Tjostheim), cover top right (Peter Elvidge), cover background (Kyle Smith), 5 (Hugo de Wolf), 11 (Mikhail Lavrenov), 13 (Prism 68), 14 (Yvan), 27 (Jan Martin Will), 40 (Tobias Machhaus), 41 (Thomas Barrat), 42 (Carolina), 45 (R. MacKay Photography).

Cover pictures: Bottom left: A flare boom burns off excess gas on an offshore oil rig. Top right: The cooling towers of a coal-fired power station. Background: Pollution pours out of a smoke stack.

Every attempt has been made to clear copyright. Should there be any inadvertent omission, please apply to the publisher for rectification.

Printed in China

1 2 3 4 5 6 7 8 9 14 13 12 11 10 09 08

Contents

CHAPTER 1

A Crisis in the Making

It is 2025. Danny is visiting the Arctic National Wildlife Refuge in Alaska with his parents. He had looked forward to the trip, reading books about the area and looking at pictures of the different animals living there, such as caribou, arctic foxes, polar bears, and snow geese. When Danny and his parents toured the area with their guide, though, they saw very few animals. "Where are they?" Danny asked. The guide shook his head sadly and explained that the Arctic National Wildlife Refuge used to be home to hundreds of species of mammals, fish, and birds. The situation changed when the U.S. government opened the area to oil and gas exploration and drilling in 2010. This created more fuel for the people of the United States, but it also upset the habitats of many animals, leading to a loss of animal life.

For thousands of years, people all over the world have depended on fossil fuels as their main source of energy. We use three types of fossil fuels: coal, oil, and natural gas. Energy from fossil fuels heats our homes, runs power plants that make electricity, and powers our cars. Fossil fuels have many advantages. They are good sources of energy, they are relatively easy to find, and they are not expensive to use. According to the U.S. Energy Information Administration, about 86 percent of the energy used in the world comes from fossil fuels.

The Problems With Fossil Fuels

In recent years, people have become aware of some serious problems with fossil fuels. One concern is that the world may be running out of them. The fossil fuels we use today were created millions of years ago. They were formed from prehistoric plants and animals, which explains how they got their name. New fossil fuels cannot be made. Once we've used them up, they will be gone forever.

Fossil fuels are not found in every part of the world, which can create problems among nations. Many countries rely on fossil fuels

that come from other countries or areas such as the Middle East, where much of the world's oil is found. Political problems in those places can interrupt the supply of fossil fuels. That can create shortages in nations far away. To get around this problem, many countries are trying to develop their own energy sources so they will not have to depend on other countries for their fuel.

At chemical plants, a fossil fuel such as oil or natural gas is converted into products like fertilizer, detergent, or rubber. Such plants may release harmful pollutants into the environment.

THE WORLD'S PRIMARY SOURCES OF ENERGY

Type of power	Quadrillion Btu*	% of total
Oil	167.50	37.5
Coal	114.51	25.6
Natural gas	103.40	23.2
Hydroelectric (water) power	27.53	6.2
Nuclear electric power	27.47	6.2
Other	6.03	1.3
TOTAL	446.44	

* Btu (British thermal unit) is a unit of energy (the amount of energy required to raise one pound of water by 1° F). A quadrillion is one thousand million million (1,000,000,000,000,000).

Source: U.S. Energy Information Administration, 2004

THE FORMATION OF FOSSIL FUELS

Fossil fuels were formed hundreds of millions of years ago. Long before dinosaurs walked Earth, much of the land was covered with swamps. The air was warm and humid, and forests of tall trees, ferns, mosses, and other plants grew. Large insects flew in the air, and primitive amphibians, reptiles, and fish lived on the land or in the water. The water was also filled with algae, a plant-like organism. When the plants and animals died, they sank to the bottom of the water. Their remains decomposed (broke down) and were covered by mud. Layers of sand, dirt and clay built up. Each layer pressed down on the layers beneath it, packing them tightly. After millions of years, the weight and pressure turned the broken-down remains of the plants and animals into coal, oil, or natural gas. Coal came from land plants, while oil and natural gas came from water plants and animals.

Millions of years ago, Earth was covered with forests containing swamps and primitive plants. The remains of these plants gave rise to the coal deposits we still use today.

Many of the processes used to mine and drill for fossil fuels can hurt the environment. Coal-fired power plants, for example, create a lot of air pollution. Oil refineries also pollute the air and produce waste that contaminates local water sources. Transporting the fuels from the places where they are made to the places where they are used can also harm the environment. Coal is transported on diesel-powered locomotives, while crude oil is usually transported by tanker ships, each of which is powered by fossil fuels. Oil spills from huge tanker ships can spoil the shoreline and harm fish and seabirds.

Fossil Fuels and Climate Change

Fossil fuels have also been linked to climate change. Burning fossil fuels produces gases, in particular carbon dioxide, that trap heat in the atmosphere. Many scientists believe that these greenhouse gases are raising global temperatures. Global warming has had numerous effects. It has led to rising sea levels around the world as glaciers melt, threatening low-lying islands and coastal settlements. The retreat of glaciers is causing habitat loss for polar wildlife. It has also resulted in landslides and flash floods in mountainous areas. Global warming has caused extreme weather conditions in many places. In others, the timing of the seasons has changed. Those changes have seriously affected agriculture. Many scientists predict that global warming will get worse unless we limit our use of fossil fuels or find ways to make them cleaner and safer.

WHAT WOULD YOU DO?

You Are in Charge
You are part of a government group that has to decide if an aging coal plant should be given a new license. What are some of the advantages and disadvantages of allowing the coal plant to continue to operate? Name at least three other energy sources that are used to generate power. See page 47 for suggestions.

CHAPTER 2

Fuels from Fossils

It is 2025. Vadim and his family are scared. They live in Donetsk, Ukraine, where Vadim's father works in a large coal mine. The mine has been the site of many fatal accidents since 1999, including one in November 2007 that left 100 miners dead. After each accident, people asked for safety improvements, but nothing was done. The mine in Donetsk is especially dangerous because it is very deep. The deeper the mine, the more hazardous it is. Since coal is becoming scarcer around the world, the mine owners are urging workers to take risks to extract as much coal as possible. Vadim's father would like to get a different job, but work is hard to find in Donetsk. He feels he has no choice but to keep working in the mine.

Finding and Using Coal

Coal is a hard black or brown material similar to rock. It is made of a number of substances, including carbon, hydrogen, oxygen, and nitrogen. Different types of coal are found at different levels in the ground. Anthracite, or hard coal, is shiny and black. It is found at the deepest level. Anthracite is mostly made of carbon. It contains much more carbon than the other types of coal, which makes anthracite a better source of energy. Above it is bituminous coal, sometimes called soft coal. Bituminous coal is the most common type of coal. The layer on top of bituminous coal is lignite, or brown coal, which is soft and crumbly.

For thousands of years people have used coal as a source of heat and energy. The Chinese are believed to have operated a coal mine in northeastern China about 3,000 years ago. In the 1200s, the Chinese burned lumps of coal for heat, as did the British, and coal fires were common in homes for many years. As time went on, people began to use coal as a power source, too. In 1709, a British iron-maker named Abraham Darby converted a wood-burning furnace so that it burned coke (a by-product of coal) instead. Burning coke turned out to be a more efficient way to produce iron. Coal also became widely used to power machines in factories — still a common use today. From the late 1800s until today, coal has been used to generate electricity.

HOW COAL FORMS

This series of photos shows the stages of coal formation and the order in which the different types of coal are found.

1

Hundreds of millions of years ago, a piece of plant matter lives and dies. Then it sinks to the bottom of a swamp. The plant matter decays and becomes peat.

2

Layers of sediment build up above the peat, squeezing it down until, after millions of years, it becomes lignite, or brown coal.

3

The action of time, heat, and pressure eventually turns lignite into an even denser material called bituminous coal.

4

As coal is compressed further and the moisture content falls, the carbon content rises. Anthracite is the hardest, most carbon-rich coal, found at the deepest levels.

FUELING THE INDUSTRIAL REVOLUTION

The Industrial Revolution marked the shift from an economy based on agriculture to one based on machines that produced goods. It began in Britain in the 1700s. By the 1850s, the Industrial Revolution had changed life in Europe and the United States. A good deal of energy was needed to run the new machines. James Watt, a Scottish inventor and engineer, designed a new type of engine that burned coal to heat water. This produced steam, which pushed a piston that turned a wheel to run the engine. Soon, coal was also powering the steamships and trains that carried the new goods from place to place.

Coal is found in every continent of the world, usually deep in the earth in strips called seams. To reach the seams, people use machines to dig vertical shafts, some up to 500 feet (153 meters) deep. Then horizontal tunnels are dug. Once the coal seams are reached, other machines are used to cut the coal from the surrounding rock.

Some seams of coal are closer to the surface, covered only by a few layers of rock and soil. These deposits are gathered in surface mines, where workers use drills and explosives to break up and strip away the layers. Surface mines can sometimes have harmful effects on the local environment, including the disruption of wildlife habitats. The displacement of soil can cause landslides and affect drainage,

Working in a coal mine can be hazardous. Miners often work deep underground and are exposed to coal dust, which can cause lung diseases. Fires, cave-ins, and explosions can also occur in the mines.

This is a surface mine for lignite (brown coal) in Germany. The lignite is burned and transformed into electricity by the power stations on the horizon.

The mining process produces waste, known as slurry. The waste often washes into local waterways, poisoning aquatic life. After the coal is mined, it is shipped in trains, trucks, or boats to power plants and factories.

Coal mining can be dangerous, with the possibility of fires and cave-ins. Explosions can occur if underground gas leaks into a mine. In February 2005, a terrible accident happened at the Sunjiwan coal mine in Fuxin, China, when an earthquake was followed by a gas explosion. More than 200 people died. Miners are also exposed to coal dust, which can cause lung diseases.

THE WORLD'S TOP TEN PRODUCERS OF HARD COAL

Rank	Country	Production (million tons)
1	China	2,736
2	United States	1,091
3	India	471
4	Australia	341
5	South Africa	267
6	Russia	257
7	Indonesia	186
8	Poland	105
9	Kazakhstan	101
10	Colombia	71

Source: World Coal Institute, 2006

Deposits of natural gas and oil are often found together. At this gas-oil-separation plant in the Shaybah oil field in Saudi Arabia, the two fuels are separated and excess gas is burned off. Then the oil can be shipped through pipelines to refineries for processing.

Finding and Using Oil and Natural Gas

Oil — sometimes called petroleum — is a thick, dark-colored liquid, while natural gas can be a vapor or a liquid. Natural gas is mostly methane, a chemical compound made of carbon and hydrogen. When prehistoric plants and animals died and decomposed, they were buried under layers of mud, sand, and rock. The layers pressed down and heated the remains, turning some

DANGER!

Natural gas is invisible and has no smell. It is very flammable, however, so leaks can be dangerous. To make sure people can tell if there is a natural gas leak, developers mix the gas with a harmless chemical that makes it smell like rotten eggs. If your house uses natural gas and you smell rotten eggs, leave the building right away. Don't use any electricity, since an electrical spark could ignite the gas. Once outside, call for emergency help.

of them into oil. Deeper down, where it was hotter, the remains turned into natural gas. Some of the oil and natural gas flowed into spaces in the surrounding rocks. People drill into those spaces to find deposits of oil and natural gas today.

Thousands of years ago, ancient people used oil and natural gas that leaked up from below the ground. Oil especially had many uses. People rubbed it on their skin as a medicine and on boats to make them waterproof. They burned oil in lamps to provide light. Natural gas may have lit the "eternal fires" of ancient people who worshipped fire.

Today, people use both oil and natural gas for heat. Oil is also used as fuel to power vehicles.

THE MANY USES OF OIL

Oil is not just used to run power plants and provide heat. Oil is also used to make:

■ Asphalt, a substance used to pave roads and make waterproofing materials

■ Fertilizer to help plants grow

■ Grease for bicycle chains and other metal parts that move

■ Fibers that are used in carpets and clothing

■ Plastic products, including soda bottles, toys, and grocery bags

■ Soap for washing dishes and clothes

Products such as these plastic bottles are made from crude oil.

Oil rigs are huge structures that hold the equipment needed to drill for oil and natural gas. Many are built offshore so they can drill for deposits under the seabed.

THE WORLD'S TOP TEN OIL PRODUCERS

Rank	Country	Production (thousand barrels per day)
1	Saudi Arabia	10,665
2	Russia	9,677
3	United States	8,330
4	Iran	4,148
5	China	3,845
6	Mexico	3,707
7	Canada	3,288
8	United Arab Emirates	2,945
9	Venezuela	2,803
10	Norway	2,786

Source: U.S. Energy Information Administration, 2006

In the 1800s, people began digging pits to bring oil up to the surface, but they could not reach the oil that was deep underground. That changed in 1859 when a retired railroad conductor named Edwin L. Drake dug the first oil well in Titusville, Pennsylvania. He used a steam-driven machine to drill 69 feet (21 meters) down into the ground to find oil and pump it to the surface. People still use Drake's basic method today. To find both oil and natural gas, people use drilling rigs to bore through levels of earth to reach the deposits. Pumping brings oil and natural gas to the surface. Since most oil and natural gas deposits are under the ocean floor, large floating platforms are built to bring them up. Huge ships called tankers carry the oil to different places. The oil must be processed at an oil refinery to turn it into the products people use.

Extracting oil and natural gas can release harmful chemicals into the air. In addition, dangerous chemicals are sometimes injected underground to increase production. Spills from oil tankers have caused numerous accidents over the years, contaminating beaches and shorelines. In one of the worst such accidents, the tanker *Exxon Valdez* ran aground off the coast of Alaska in March 1989, spilling 11 million gallons (42 million liters) of crude oil. The spill killed hundreds of thousands of fish, seabirds, and other animals and did great environmental damage. Proposals to build offshore natural gas terminals have raised concerns because of fears of accidental leaks, fires, and explosions.

After a cargo ship carrying oil struck a bridge in California's San Francisco Bay in 2007, it spilled fuel in the water and contaminated many miles of shore. Birds like this one were covered with oil and struggled to clean themselves. Thousands of birds died.

WHAT WOULD YOU DO?

You Are in Charge
You work for an international organization that supports the protection of wildlife around the world. You are going to take part in a debate with the spokesperson from the oil and gas industry. He will argue in favor of opening certain wildlife refuges to oil and gas exploration. What points do you want to make in the debate?

CHAPTER 3

Running Short

It is 2025. Olivia is trying to do her homework by candlelight on yet another cold, dark night. Olivia lives in Buffalo, New York. Like much of the United States, Buffalo has been hit by periodic blackouts during the last few months. Not enough oil or gas is available to run the power plants. Olivia must pull branches off the trees in the garden to stock her home's wood-burning stove, which her family depends on for heat and for cooking. She is grumpy and bored because she cannot watch television or use her computer. Her parents warn her that the blackouts will probably continue. Conditions are not expected to improve in the near future.

A Growing Population

The world's population is growing rapidly. At the beginning of 2008, there were more than 6.7 billion people. That number is expected to top 8 billion by 2030. More people means demand for goods, services, and supplies will also increase. Many vital resources, including fossil fuels, are being used at a faster rate than ever before.

Energy demands around the world are growing at an alarming rate. The International Energy Agency (IEA) estimates that by 2030, the world's energy needs will be more than 50 percent greater than they are today.

Many people oppose the development of oil fields in Alaska because of the environmental damage it may cause. At a rally in Washington, D.C., in 2005, protesters called for a ban on oil exploration in the Arctic Wildlife Refuge.

Many experts believe that there are not enough fossil fuels to meet the need. Fossil fuels are being used up quickly. As they are not renewable resources, once they are gone, they are gone forever. Estimates vary, but geologists and engineers suggest that, using current methods of mining and extraction, oil may run out in the next 100 years. Coal and natural gas may run out in about 200 years.

RISING ENERGY DEMANDS

The world's demand for energy has grown steadily and, according to projections, the demand will continue to grow.

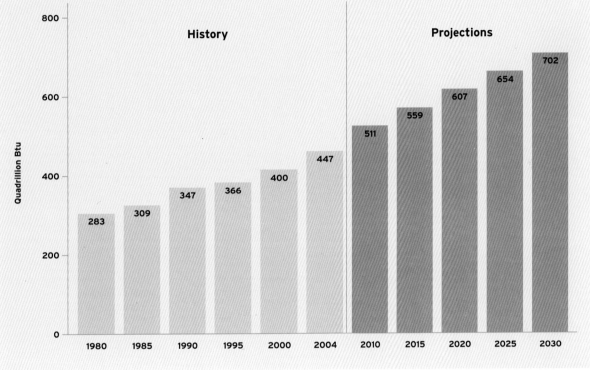

Source: U.S. Energy Information Administration

New Sources of Old Fuels

To make sure we do not run out of fossil fuels, efforts are underway to find new sources. Many billions of tons of coal still exist underground, especially in the United States, Russia, China, and India. Improved methods of exploration could lead to the discovery of even more coal. New mining techniques could enable the coal industry to get to deposits that once could not be reached.

Vast quantities of oil and natural gas exist in new or untapped fields. Alaska is a prime source of such fields in the United States. The federal government approved oil exploration in a new field on the coastal plain of northern Alaska near the town of Kaktovik, as well as oil and natural gas development off the coast in the Chukchi Sea. Development of both sites is controversial, however, because it might disrupt the habitats of polar bears and other animals.

Kashagan, another huge oil field, was discovered in 2000 in Kazakhstan, under the Caspian Sea. By 2008, production at Kashagan had still not begun because developing the field is difficult. The oil is located 2.5 miles (4 kilometers) beneath the seabed, in a very cold region. The field also contains a great deal of natural gas. Dangerous sulphur is present, too, which adds to the difficulties of developing the field.

Late in 2007, another important underwater oil field, called Tupi, was discovered off the coast of Brazil. Brazil's national oil company faced significant challenges in developing the field. Tupi lies about 4.5 miles (7.2 kilometers) below the surface of the ocean, and developers would have to drill through miles of sand, rock, and salt to reach it. Getting the oil to shore requires installing pipes that can be kept warm and that are strong enough to resist being worn away by the salt.

Oil sands (also called tar sands) are another new source of oil. The largest deposits are in Canada, Venezuela, and the Middle East. Oil sands contain a heavy form of crude oil that is in solid or semi-solid form. Processing oil sands uses up a great deal of water and energy. This could be a problem in areas where water is not readily available.

While exploring for oil, scientists from a French company conduct investigations of the Caspian Sea. A huge oil field has been discovered under the seabed in Kazakhstan.

Another new source of oil is oil shale. This is a rock that produces a substance similar to oil when it is heated using a special chemical process. Extracting oil from oil shale is more difficult than extracting conventional oil.

The Nuclear Option

One alternative to using fossil fuels is nuclear power. Nuclear plants produce reliable energy without many of the environmental problems associated with burning fossil fuels. Nuclear power is popular in parts of Europe, supplying 80 percent of the electricity in France.

Nuclear plants have drawbacks. Operating the plants requires a great deal of water, which could be a problem if there is a drought. Accidents or leaks at a plant could release harmful substances into the surrounding area. The plants also produce radioactive waste, which remains radioactive, and therefore harmful to life, for thousands of years. Nuclear plants must take great care when disposing of radioactive waste. Most of the waste is in the form of large metal rods that give off dangerous radiation. A permanent solution is needed for how and where to store nuclear waste – possibly deep underground.

Oil sands, a tar-like substance, are a promising new source of oil. The material must be processed to produce crude oil. This sample is from Alberta, Canada, where some of the largest deposits of oil sands are found.

WHAT WOULD YOU DO?

You Are in Charge

Your city council is holding a meeting on whether to build a nuclear power plant. You think that this is a good idea because, unlike power plants that burn fossil fuels, nuclear plants do not generate air pollution. How will you argue against the following points, which will be raised by opponents of nuclear power?

- An accident at a nuclear power plant could cause the release of dangerous radiation throughout the area.
- A nuclear power plant could become the target of a terrorist attack.
- There is no long-range plan for the disposal of nuclear waste.

CHAPTER 4

Global Interconnections

It is 2025. Tom has been waiting in line for hours at a gas station, trying to buy fuel for his car. There is a severe gas shortage in the United States, brought on by a conflict in the Middle East that disrupted oil shipments. When drivers can get gas, it costs $10 per gallon. Violence is breaking out among frustrated drivers. Cities and towns can't get enough fuel to run buses, and many people can't get to work or school. Increased transportation costs have also caused the price of food and other merchandise to go up. People are angry and unhappy. Government leaders don't know how to solve the crisis.

Meeting Our Energy Needs

The energy world is complicated, with many countries forced to import fuel from other nations. Imagine how much simpler things would be if, say, the United States could produce all the energy it needs. If that were the case, the United States would not have to worry about getting fuel from other nations. Like most countries, though, the United States does not produce enough fuel to meet its energy needs.

Other countries also import much of the fuel they need. European countries get more than one-fourth of their natural gas from Russia. Some Eastern European countries depend on Russia for almost all of their natural gas.

These interconnections mean that political, social, economic, and environmental events in one country can have a major impact on the supply of fuel to another country half a world away.

The Supply of Oil and Natural Gas

In 1960, some of the world's top oil producers formed the Organization of Petroleum Exporting Countries (OPEC). Today, OPEC produces nearly half of the world's oil. The group is led by Saudi Arabia, which is the world's top oil exporter. OPEC members

meet regularly to decide whether to increase or decrease the amount of oil they produce. That decision affects the amount of oil available worldwide, as well as the price. As of July 2008, oil reached as much as $147 a barrel for the first time. Oil cost only $20 a barrel in late 2001.

Protesters demonstrated across Nepal after the government sharply raised fuel prices in January 2008. After two days of protests that disrupted the country, the government announced that the prices would not be increased.

THE PRICE OF A GALLON OF GAS

The price of a gallon of gas differs around the world. Consumers in some European countries pay much more per gallon than consumers in the United States. This chart shows the average retail cost of a gallon of gas in several different countries in July 2008.

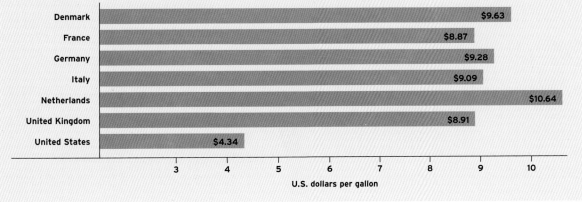

Country	Price
Denmark	$9.63
France	$8.87
Germany	$9.28
Italy	$9.09
Netherlands	$10.64
United Kingdom	$8.91
United States	$4.34

U.S. dollars per gallon

Source: U.S. Energy Information Administration

21

Much of the world's oil comes from the Middle East, a region troubled by war and political tensions that often threaten the oil supply. Political instability also exists in other oil-producing areas, including Africa and South America.

Russia is the world's largest exporter of natural gas. The fuel is shipped to consumers in Europe and elsewhere, mostly through pipelines that cross Ukraine. In early 2006, the Ukrainian government had a dispute with Gazprom, Russia's government-controlled energy company. Gazprom cut Ukraine's natural gas supply, which led to shortages across Europe in the middle of winter.

Since it relies so much on Russia for its fuel, the European Union has tried to find other supplies of natural gas. One possibility is the planned construction of the Nabucco gas pipeline, which would run from Turkey to Austria and carry natural gas to Europe from the Middle East.

THE OIL EMBARGO OF 1973

In October 1973, Arab countries in the Middle East imposed an embargo (a government restriction on trade) on oil, stopping shipments to the United States and other nations. The Arab countries were angry because the United States was supporting Israel during a war with Egypt and Syria and they wanted to persuade the United States to change its policies. The oil embargo lasted until March 1974. It resulted in fuel shortages, price increases, and driving restrictions.

Demand Around the World

Rising demand also affects the supply of fuel. Developed countries consume the most fuel. However, there has been a recent surge in demand from the large industrializing nations of China and India. Meanwhile, there has been growing demand from people in the oil-exporting nations themselves. That means they have less fuel to sell abroad. If demand in oil-producing nations continues to grow, many of these countries might need to import oil themselves.

Trying to Achieve Energy Independence

For years, people in the United States have urged the country to work toward energy independence. Supporters of energy independence say that the United States would be stronger and more secure if the country did not have to rely on other nations for its energy. They call for the development of more home-based oil and natural gas, as well as seeking alternatives to traditional fossil fuels within the United States.

Government leaders met in 2005 to open the Blue Stream gas pipeline, which carries natural gas from Russia to Turkey through the Black Sea. Shown from left to right are Vladimir Putin (Russian president, 2000-2008), Recep Tayyip Erdogan (Turkish prime minister since 2003), and Silvio Berlusconi (prime minister of Italy, 2001-2006 and since 2008).

WHAT WOULD YOU DO?

You Are in Charge

You work for an organization that encourages people to lead more environmentally-friendly lives. You are in charge of an advertising campaign to convince people to explore alternatives to driving their own cars to work. How can you convince people to walk, take a bus or train, share a car, or ride a bicycle? How can you convince companies to allow their employees to work from home?

CHAPTER 5

The Climate Connection

It is 2025. Peter, an Inuit, is working on an oil rig at the North Pole. Years ago such work was impossible, but as a result of global warming the ice cap in the Arctic region has melted. This has given developers access to about 25 percent of Earth's oil resources that were previously unreachable. Peter's job is dangerous, and the rig is often shut down because several countries are fighting over who has the right to drill in the area.

Peter has other worries as well. The melting ice caused sea levels to rise all over the world. That flooded coastal communities around the Arctic Ocean, including the village where his family lives. Peter has no choice but to work on the dangerous rig, spending months away from his family. Other work is scarce, especially since the polar bears and walruses that he used to hunt are becoming extinct, victims of the destruction of their icy habitat.

The images are frightening: a world where temperatures are rising, glaciers are melting, forest fires are raging, and river beds are drying up. According to many scientists, such developments will occur unless people take steps to halt global warming. One of the main ways to combat global warming is to move away from the use of fossil fuels.

A heavy blanket of smog hangs over Santiago, Chile, one of the world's most polluted cities. The smog in Santiago is primarily caused by automobile emissions and the burning of fossil fuels by factories.

Fossil Fuels and Pollution

When we burn fossil fuels, it damages the quality of the air we breathe and affects our health. The sources can be car engines, coal-fired power plants, and mines. When burned, fossil fuels produce pollutants such as carbon dioxide, carbon monoxide, and nitrogen dioxide. Those

pollutants can cause headaches, lung damage, pneumonia, asthma, and other respiratory problems. They also lead to the formation of smog — the thick, dirty fog that hangs over such crowded cities as Beijing, China; Los Angeles, California; Athens, Greece; and Mexico City, Mexico.

The burning of fossil fuels has also been linked to acid rain. When the fuels are burned, the fumes they produce contain such things as nitrogen and sulfur. Those chemicals rise into the air, where they are absorbed into the water drops that make up clouds. There they mix with other chemicals to form substances that have high acid levels. Those substances then fall back to Earth in the form of acid rain (as well as acid snow and fog). Acid rain damages rivers, lakes, plants, animals, crops, and even buildings and cars.

This forest on Mount Mitchell in North Carolina has been heavily damaged by acid rain. The acids have had a particularly bad effect on spruce and fir trees.

Global Warming and the Greenhouse Effect

Perhaps even more worrying is the connection between fossil fuels and global warming. Global warming is an increase in the temperature of Earth's atmosphere, seas, and land, leading to widespread changes in the climate. Earth is currently undergoing a period of warming brought on largely by human activities — especially the use of fossil fuels.

How does the warming take place? It has to do with a phenomenon called the greenhouse effect, which occurs naturally on Earth. The Sun's rays heat the land and seas, but much of the heat bounces back off Earth's surface. Some of this heat is absorbed by gases, water vapor, and particles in the atmosphere, preventing it from escaping — a bit like the way heat is trapped within the glass walls of a greenhouse. When the greenhouse effect works the way it should — as it

This diagram shows how the greenhouse effect works. Earth's surface absorbs some of the Sun's heat while the rest reflects back into space. The build-up of gases such as carbon dioxide in the atmosphere causes more of the Sun's heat to become trapped, leading to global warming.

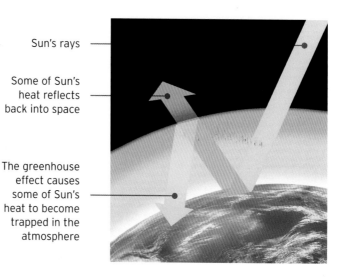

Sun's rays

Some of Sun's heat reflects back into space

The greenhouse effect causes some of Sun's heat to become trapped in the atmosphere

GREENHOUSE GAS EMISSIONS OF SELECTED COUNTRIES

This chart shows emissions of energy-related carbon dioxide in million metric tons for 1990 and 2004, with projections for later years.

Country	1990	2004	2010	2020	2030
Brazil	220	334	403	500	597
Canada	474	584	648	694	750
China	2,241	4,707	6,497	8,795	11,239
India	578	1,111	1,283	1,720	2,156
Japan	1,015	1,262	1,274	1,294	1,306
Mexico	300	385	481	592	699
Russia	2,334	1,685	1,809	2,018	2,185
United States	4,989	5,923	6,214	6,944	7,950

Source: U.S. Energy Information Administration

has for millions of years — it helps sustain life and keep Earth's temperature comfortable.

Over the last 150 years, however, the greenhouse effect has been intensified. Human activities, including the increased use of fossil fuels, have released much larger amounts of greenhouse gases into the atmosphere. These gases trap more of the Sun's energy and cause global warming. Carbon dioxide is the most important greenhouse gas. Large amounts of carbon dioxide are released when fossil fuels are burned.

Developed nations, such as the United States and the countries of the European Union, emit more carbon dioxide and other greenhouse gases than developing nations. In fact, the United States is the world's greatest producer of greenhouse gases. This is because it is the world's greatest consumer of fossil fuels, despite having only five percent of the world's population. By 2010, China is expected to overtake the United States as the leading producer of greenhouse gases. China has the world's largest population and uses a great deal of coal to power its plants.

Polar bears are among the animals most threatened by global warming. If the ice in polar regions continues to melt, as scientists fear it will, polar bears would have to change the way they live and eat to survive.

Temperatures Rising

The average surface temperature of Earth has risen steadily over the years. In the 20th century, the temperature rose approximately 1° Fahrenheit. This may not sound like much, but an increase of just a few degrees can have a dramatic effect. During the last Ice Age (which ended around 10,000 years ago), the temperature was only 5° F to 9° F (2.7° C to 5° C) colder than it is today. Yet it caused huge ice sheets that covered much of North America, Europe, and Asia.

According to scientists at the National Aeronautics and Space Administration (NASA) and the National Oceanic and Atmospheric Administration, 2007 was one of the warmest years on record. In fact, nine of the ten warmest years on record have occurred since 1997. Unless something is done to slow global warming, the temperature is expected to continue to increase.

These people make their way through the flooded streets of Dhaka, Bangladesh, after the country was hit by heavy floods in July 2007. Climate scientists fear that global warming will cause sea levels to rise, resulting in permanent flooding in certain parts of the world.

GLOBAL RISE IN TEMPERATURE

This chart shows the changes in Earth's average surface temperature that have taken place over time, from 1860 to 2000. Temperatures have risen steadily since 1980.

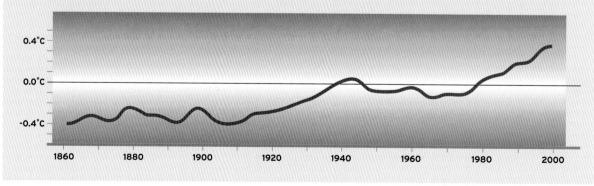

Source: Intergovernmental Panel on Climate Change

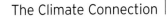

The Muir Glacier retreats at Glacier Bay National Park in Alaska. Between 1941 and 2004 the glacier retreated more than 7.5 miles (12 kilometers) and thinned by over 2,625 feet (800 meters), due to global warming. The melting has formed a glacial lake, which has filled the valley, replacing the ice.

Climate scientists predict devastating effects unless global warming is stopped. The oceans could rise, causing severe flooding in coastal areas. Snow cover could decrease in Arctic regions, and ice and mountain glaciers could disappear. Different places could see weather extremes, including heat waves, droughts, ice storms, and heavy rainfall.

POSSIBLE EFFECTS OF GLOBAL WARMING

The United Nations Intergovernmental Panel on Climate Change reports that global warming could have the following effects:

- Rising temperatures of the air and seas
- Rising levels of the seas, and as a result, more frequent flooding
- In Arctic regions, a decrease in snow cover, melting of ice, disappearance of mountain glaciers, and thawing of the permafrost (the underlying soil or rock that is permanently frozen)
- An increase in precipitation (rain or snow) in certain regions, as well as an increase in the frequency of extreme precipitation in some areas
- More intense and longer droughts in other regions
- A greater frequency of heat waves
- A greater chance of ice storms, leaving people without power for extended periods of time
- A decline in and extinction of some plant and animal species

AN EARLY WARNING

The idea that increased levels of carbon dioxide in the air could cause Earth to warm is not new. The theory was first suggested in 1895 by a Swedish chemist named Svante Arrhenius. Arrhenius presented a paper to a scientific society stating that increasing or decreasing the amount of carbon dioxide in the atmosphere would raise or lower the temperature of Arctic regions. He also estimated how much effect burning fossil fuels would have on temperature. "We are evaporating our coal mines into the air," he wrote. Arrhenius was awarded the Nobel Prize in Chemistry in 1903 for work that was unrelated to climate science. In fact, he considered climate science his hobby, not his main work.

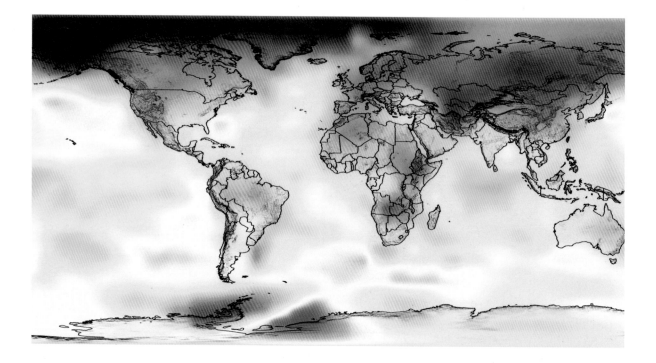

Many of the warnings on global warming have come from the Intergovernmental Panel on Climate Change (IPCC). The group was created in 1988 by the United Nations Environment Programme and the World Meteorological Organization to investigate climate change. The IPCC has issued regular reports over the years that have collected the most recent work of climate scientists. The reports have told the world what to expect if global warming continues. They have also suggested ways to address the problem.

This map shows changes in average global temperatures from 2002 to 2006, with a scale ranging from dark red to blue. The orange and red areas had temperatures that were warmer than average, while the blue areas had colder-than-average temperatures. Yellow areas experienced average temperatures.

One of the IPCC's early reports and other research findings were discussed in 1992, when the United Nations met in Rio de Janeiro, Brazil. Nearly 200 nations signed an agreement in Rio to reduce emissions of carbon dioxide and other greenhouse gases. The treaty did not include specific deadlines or targets for cutting emissions. However, it was the first coordinated effort to stop climate change.

In 2007, the IPCC and Al Gore, the former vice president of the United States, won the Nobel Peace Prize for their work in spreading knowledge about climate change. Gore became an activist on environmental issues following his defeat in the 2000 presidential election. In 2006, Gore starred in a documentary about global warming called *An Inconvenient Truth*, which won two Academy Awards. He has also written a number of books about the environment and travels the world, speaking about climate change and other environmental issues.

Al Gore (left) and Rajendra Pachauri, the head of the IPCC, display their diplomas and gold medals after receiving the Nobel Peace Prize in Oslo, Norway, in 2007. When Gore arrived in Oslo, he did not take a traditional motorcade from the airport. Instead, he opted for the environmentally-friendly airport train, then walked from the train station to his hotel.

WHAT WOULD YOU DO?

You Are in Charge

You are working on a documentary on climate change. You need to decide what to include in the documentary. What points do you want to focus on and what images will you select to make them? What locations do you want to shoot in?

CHAPTER 6

Taking the First Steps

It is 2025. Shen lives with his family in Guangzhou in southeastern China. Guangzhou is a crowded, busy city, full of factories. The air is heavy with fumes from the millions of motorcycles, cars, and trucks that fill the streets. Guangzhou and the rest of China have changed over the last 20 years. Many power plants have been built and coal consumption has doubled throughout the country. These efforts have helped China become more modern and industrialized, which has improved the standard of living but has harmed people's health. Breathing can be so difficult that Shen and his family must wear masks when they are outside. In fact, they try not to leave the house unless they have to. If they do open the windows, everything in their house gets covered in a layer of soot.

Deciding what to do about global warming is not easy, especially when any action we take involves changing the way we live. For example, we would need to reduce our use of, or even stop using, the fuels that make our cars run and produce electricity. It is hard for people to agree to make changes in their daily lives. It may be even harder for governments to agree to change their nations' policies and

Cleaners sweep the road during a dust storm in Beijing, China, in 2006. The dust is loose soil that has blown in from a growing desert area in northwest China. The dust picks up harmful emissions from factories and power plants on its way into the city. Breathing the dust can cause sore throats and respiratory problems. City officials advise people not to go out on days like this without wearing a mask.

practices. Nevertheless, many world leaders have taken the first steps to try to halt global warming.

The Kyoto Protocol

In December 1997, delegates representing more than 150 nations went to Kyoto, Japan, for a meeting called by the United Nations. Their job was to come up with an international treaty to deal with climate change. The treaty, called the Kyoto Protocol, set detailed limits on the amount of carbon dioxide and other greenhouse gases that certain countries could produce.

This woman and her grandchildren, who live in Karnataka, India, were given 150 mango tree saplings as part of a program to reduce overall emissions of carbon dioxide. The trees absorb carbon dioxide in the atmosphere that has been emitted by polluters.

MAIN POINTS OF THE KYOTO PROTOCOL

- Between 2008 and 2012, 38 industrialized nations have to cut their greenhouse gas emissions to 5 percent below the levels they produced in 1990.

- Developing countries should set voluntary targets for cutting their greenhouse gas emissions.

The Protocol was criticized by some politicians and activists. There were complaints that it did not include developing nations in the list of countries that had to cut their emissions. China and India — the countries with the world's largest populations — did not have to make cuts. Both countries have undergone large-scale industrialization in recent times. They are heavy polluters, burning large quantities of fossil fuels. India and China also planned to build hundreds of new coal-fired power plants.

U.S. President George W. Bush announced in 2001 that the United States would not be part of the agreement. He said it would hurt

Delegates take part in a session of the U.N. Framework Convention on Climate Change in December 2007. The meeting, in Bali, Indonesia, was called to discuss a new international treaty to cut emissions of greenhouse gases.

U.S. industry. Other large nations did approve the agreement, however, including the members of the European Union (E.U.) in 2002 and Russia in 2004. The Kyoto Protocol went into effect in February 2005.

Climate Talks in Bali

The Kyoto Protocol expires in 2012. A new treaty to cut emissions of greenhouse gases is needed to replace it. Delegates from more than 180 countries met in Bali, Indonesia, in December 2007 to discuss how to tackle the problem. After two weeks of heated discussions, the delegates agreed that deep cuts in global emissions were needed to deal with climate change. They called for action on the part of both industrialized and developing nations. It was the first time that developing countries agreed to work toward making definite cuts in emissions. A new treaty should be in place by late 2009.

MAIN POINTS OF THE BALI AGREEMENT

- Industrialized nations would take steps to deal with climate change. These steps include setting targets for cutting emissions, but no specific targets or goals were set.
- Developing nations would also agree to cut their emissions.
- Industrialized nations would help poorer developing countries cut their emissions by giving them financial and technological aid.
- The Intergovernmental Panel on Climate Change (IPCC) urged industrialized countries to cut their greenhouse gas emissions to 25-40 percent of their 1990 levels by the year 2020.

The European Union Acts

In 2005, the E.U. took the lead in cutting greenhouse gas emissions. Power plants, factories, refineries, and other polluters are told how much greenhouse gas they can emit. In 2007, the E.U. called on its members to make a 20 percent cut in greenhouse gas emissions from 1990 levels by the year 2020. As part of the plan, 20 percent of all energy was to come from renewable sources by that date.

The United States Passes New Energy Law

The United States passed a major energy law in December 2007 to help combat global warming. The law set stricter standards for manufacturers to make new cars and light trucks more fuel-efficient. By 2020, the average fuel standard for all vehicles would have to

Earthracer is a 24-meter (79-foot) trimaran racing boat, built in 2007 by New Zealand-born marine engineer Craig Loomis. It is powered by biodiesel, a fuel made from vegetable oils or animal fats.

increase to 35 miles per gallon (6.7 liters per 100 kilometers). The previous standard was 27.5 miles per gallon (8.6 liters per 100 kilometers) for cars and 22.2 miles per gallon (10.6 liters per 100 kilometers) for minivans, sport utility vehicles (SUVs), and light trucks. Under another part of the law, federal buildings and household appliances also had to be more fuel-efficient.

The law also called for an increase in the use of biofuels, such as ethanol. Those are fuels made from biological material such as corn, which can be used in vehicles in place of gasoline. The law was expected to reduce oil consumption in the United States by about 2.8 million barrels (334 million liters) per day by the year 2020, and 5 million barrels (596 million liters) per day by 2030.

Arnold Schwarzenegger, the governor of California, announces the California Hydrogen Highway Network. The plan calls for the building of special pumps throughout the state so that drivers can fill their hydrogen-fueled cars.

CALIFORNIA'S GREEN GOVERNOR

Arnold Schwarzenegger (1947–) was born in Austria. He first became famous as a bodybuilder, then as an actor. In 2003, he was elected governor of California. Since then he has led efforts to improve the state's environmental policies. In 2006, the governor signed the first law in the United States to establish a program to limit greenhouse gas emissions from major industries. He also ordered the state government to cut its energy use by 20 percent, helped set up a center to study energy efficiency, and expanded the market for alternative fuels in California. Schwarzenegger also signed an agreement with the leaders of four other states aimed at cutting greenhouse gas emissions. By 2020, one-third of California's electricity will come from renewable sources.

Developing Better Vehicles

The automobile industry has been working hard to develop more fuel-efficient vehicles. These use less gasoline and emit fewer greenhouse gases. They are also developing new types of vehicles that run on different power sources. Some of these vehicles already exist — such as cars that can run on both gasoline and biofuel — and more will be introduced in the coming years.

This futuristic vehicle from Honda runs on both gas and an electric battery. When the car runs on gas, the battery charges. When the gas is low, the engine switches to battery power. The fuel-efficient car can travel 62 miles (100 km) on a little more than half a gallon (2.36 liters) of gas.

FUEL EFFICIENCY OF DIFFERENT 2008 VEHICLES

Type of Vehicle	Model Name	Miles per gallon	
		City	Highway
Compact Car	Ford Focus	24	33
Mid-size Car	Pontiac Grand Prix	18	28
Minivan	Honda Odyssey	16	23
SUV	Chevrolet Tahoe	14	20
Hybrid	Toyota Prius	48	45

Source: U.S. Department of Energy, using Environmental Protection Agency 2008 estimates

Hybrid cars run on a combination of power sources. Most hybrids have both a gas engine and an electric motor powered by batteries.

Electric and hydrogen-powered cars exist, but they are not that common. Electric cars run on a set of batteries that power an electric motor. The cars produce very little pollution but generally cannot go very far before the batteries need to be recharged. Hydrogen cars are powered by fuel cells that run on hydrogen. When hydrogen is burned, it emits only water vapor, so it is completely clean. Before hydrogen cars can become widespread, a network of hydrogen filling stations would be needed. Hydrogen fuel cells are also being developed that could generate electricity, provide heat, and fuel airplanes.

These people are learning how to fuel a hydrogen-powered bus. They are taking part in the Hydrogen Fuel Cell Program run by AC Transit, a public bus system in California. As part of the project, AC Transit is running several zero-emission buses that are fueled partly by a hydrogen power system.

WHAT WOULD YOU DO?

You Are in Charge

You work for a branch of the United Nations that is involved with climate change. You will be meeting with government representatives from India, a country with a large population that has been developing rapidly. As the population increases so does the number of vehicles on the country's roads. What suggestions could you make to government officials to help India meet its growing transportation needs?

CHAPTER 7

Looking to the Future

It is 2025. Katie and Jacob are excited. The two college students have just won a contest to develop new vehicle technologies. The global contest is part of the Vehicle Design Summit (VDS), which began as a project organized by students at the Massachusetts Institute of Technology in 2006. Since then, VDS participants have achieved many breakthroughs. Katie and Jacob developed a car that runs entirely on a clean biofuel made from algae. Algae is a good energy source since it grows quickly and takes up less space than conventional energy crops. Manufacturers are already deciding where to plant algae farms to produce this exciting new fuel.

Developing alternative energy sources might help solve some of the problems associated with fossil fuels. Unlike fossil fuels, alternative energy sources don't produce carbon dioxide and other greenhouse gases and will not run out. These sources are more expensive than fossil fuels, however, and the supply may not be as steady or reliable.

The Power of the Sun

Sunlight contains huge amounts of energy. Solar power is clean and renewable energy that can be harnessed and put to practical use. Special panels placed on the roofs of buildings contain photovoltaic cells, which collect sunlight and convert it into heat and electricity. However, photovoltaic cells are expensive to produce. Since there is no sunlight at night or on cloudy days, solar power systems must also be able to store power for use when the sun is not shining.

In solar power plants, panels like the ones shown here are covered with photovoltaic cells. The panels collect sunlight and convert it into electricity.

The Three Gorges Dam spans the Yangtze River in China. The hydroelectric power plant is not yet fully operational, but it may some day generate enough electricity to help meet China's growing need for power.

Despite those problems, solar power is already in use throughout the world. Engineers are developing more efficient technologies that could make solar power less expensive.

Blowing in the Wind

Wind provides a good source of energy in windy areas, often along coastlines and on mountains. Wind turbines (windmill-like structures that convert wind energy into electrical power) are already used as a power source in much of Europe. Wind power generates about 20 percent of the electricity in Denmark, about 8 percent in Spain, and 5 percent in Germany. In some areas, people have built their own wind turbines to generate power for their homes, farms, or businesses.

RUSHING WATER

People have used water power for thousands of years. Today's hydroelectric systems harness the energy of moving water from waves and dams to run machines that generate electricity. Hydroelectric stations located in the ocean have little impact on the environment. "Wave farms" near the coast, however, can interfere with fish. Stations that involve building dams or diverting rivers can also cause environmental problems.

Wind turbines are relatively inexpensive to build. Wind power does not cause pollution, but it is somewhat unreliable, since the wind does not always blow strongly or when there is high demand for electricity. Many people also find the turbines unattractive and noisy and say they spoil the view. Wind farms can cause erosion if they are located in desert areas and may harm birds and bats.

Sleek wind turbines like these, which do not produce pollution, are popular power sources in much of Europe. Some people are opposed to wind farms because they find the structures unattractive and noisy.

The Debate Over Biofuels

Biofuels are made from biological materials such as corn, soy, sugarcane, seaweed, and even animal waste. Ethanol is the best known biofuel in the United States. Generally made from corn, it is used as a fuel for vehicles, either alone or mixed with gasoline.

There is a debate about whether biofuels are good or bad for the environment. Burning biofuels causes only small emissions of carbon dioxide and other greenhouse gases, which may be balanced out by the carbon that the plants absorb when they grow. Manufacturing certain types of biofuels, however, may have harmful

GEOTHERMAL POWER

Geothermal power uses heat energy that comes from deep inside Earth. Geothermal power plants extract steam or hot water to make electricity. They are popular in such places as Iceland, where volcanoes, hot springs, and geysers create heat underground. Iceland gets more than a quarter of its electricity from geothermal sources. Geothermal energy is very clean and provides a steady stream of power.

effects. For example, manufacturing ethanol requires large amounts of land, water, and fertilizer (which is made from fossil fuels), as well as energy that often comes from fossil fuels. Because producing ethanol consumes fossil fuels, many experts do not see it as an environmentally-friendly energy source. Ethanol production may also have an effect on food prices. As farmers plant more corn for ethanol, they plant fewer food crops, which can drive the price of food up.

There are also problems with some of the biofuels used in Europe. Most of the biofuels used there come from rapeseed oil (also called canola oil), but Europe also imports fuel made from palm and soybean oil. Tropical forests and other native vegetation are often cut down to plant those crops. That can destroy natural habitats and the species that live there.

Brazil developed a successful ethanol industry using sugarcane. In fact, Brazil is the largest consumer of plant-based biofuels in the world. Relatively little energy is needed to grow sugarcane and process it into fuel. In late 2007, Britain announced plans to build a plant on the south coast of Wales that would generate electricity from wood chips. The plant was expected to produce enough clean energy to power half the homes in Wales. Meanwhile, scientists are working to create biofuels from sources that might prove friendly to the environment, including algae and nuts.

At the coal-fired Ferrybridge Power Station in Yorkshire, England, rapeseed oil, from these rape plants, is used to produce biofuels. Ferrybridge is a leader in "co-fired renewable energy," using a combination of traditional and renewable fuels.

THINGS YOU CAN DO TO SAVE ENERGY

- Recycle paper, cans, and plastic products. Recycling cuts down on the energy used to produce such items. It also saves fossil fuels, as plastic products are made from oil.

- Turn off the lights when you leave a room.

- Turn off appliances when they're not in use.

- In the winter, turn down the thermostat and wear a sweater. In the summer, raise the temperature on the air conditioner.

- Walk, ride your bike, or take public transportation instead of using the family car.

- Use new compact fluorescent lightbulbs instead of traditional incandescent bulbs. CFLs last about ten times longer than traditional bulbs and use only a quarter of the electricity.

- Ask your parents to drive a more fuel-efficient car.

Making Fossil Fuels Better

People are working on ways to make fossil fuels cleaner. Making power plants more efficient, for instance, reduces the amount of carbon dioxide they emit. "Clean coal" is coal that has been treated in order to reduce the harmful effects of burning it. Clean coal technologies could help to reduce the amount of carbon dioxide emitted from coal-fired power plants. One clean coal method

At this plant in Louisiana, solid coal is exposed to high temperatures and pressure. That produces an alternative energy source called syngas. Syngas is a mixture of hydrogen and carbon monoxide. It can be used to generate power and produces fewer emissions than burning regular coal.

captures the carbon dioxide and pumps it underground. Another technique removes much of the carbon dioxide before the coal is burned. The coal is heated under pressure until it produces mostly carbon monoxide and hydrogen. Scientists are also working on using some of the same methods to capture and store carbon dioxide that is emitted by oil and natural gas plants.

Conserving Energy

Governments, corporations, and scientists have to set the policies, take the steps, and develop the technologies to deal with the problems associated with fossil fuels. All of us, though, can do our part by conserving energy. If you set your thermostat 2° F (1° C) lower in the winter and raise the setting on your air conditioner the same amount in the summer, it could save about 2,000 pounds (907 kilograms) of carbon dioxide each year. If everyone in the United States drove one of the most fuel-efficient vehicle models, it would save more than 20 billion gallons (76 billion liters) of gas in ten years.

Using compact fluorescent lightbulbs (CFLs) is a good way to save energy.

WHAT WOULD YOU DO?

You Are in Charge
Think about your "carbon footprint" – the amount of carbon dioxide that is emitted as a result of your activities. Think about what you and your family do in a typical day and week. You can calculate your emissions at this web site:

www.epa.gov/climatechange/emissions/ind_calculator.html

What steps can you take to use less energy and reduce your carbon footprint?

Glossary

acid rain Rain containing acidic substances that damage the environment, including rivers, lakes, and vegetation

algae Plant-like organisms without true leaves, roots, and stems, which grow mainly in the water

alternative energy Energy from natural sources such as the Sun, wind, and waves; such sources are renewable

biofuel A fuel produced from biological material, such as plant or animal matter

blackout A loss of electrical power due to a failure of the electricity supply

carbon dioxide A colorless, odorless gas in the atmosphere, which is a mixture of carbon and oxygen; people and animals breathe out carbon dioxide, while plants absorb it

carbon footprint A measure of the amount of carbon dioxide emitted as a result of the daily activities of an individual or organization

climate change The process of long-term changes in the world's climate

compact fluorescent lightbulb (CFL) A fluorescent lightbulb that is more energy-efficient and lasts longer than a traditional incandescent lightbulb

crude oil Oil that has not yet been refined

developed countries Relatively wealthy and technologically advanced countries that have sophisticated manufacturing and service industries

developing countries Relatively poor, non-industrialized countries whose economies are based mainly on agriculture and the exploitation of primary resources

drilling rig The equipment used for drilling for oil, including the large platform that supports the drilling equipment

embargo An official order restricting or prohibiting commerce, especially trade, with a particular nation

emission A substance that is emitted, or given off, such as a gas

ethanol A biofuel often made from corn or sugarcane

European Union (E.U.) An economic and political community of 27 member states (as of 2008) located primarily in Europe

export To send products to another country for sale

extraction The process of obtaining something from a source, usually by separating it from another material

fertilizer A chemical mixture used to add nutrients to soil in order to promote the growth of plants

flammable Capable of catching fire easily

fossil fuels Fuels (such as coal, oil, and natural gas) that come from the fossilized remains of prehistoric plants and animals; fossil fuels are not renewable and contribute to global warming

fuel cell An energy cell; a device that generates electricity by converting the chemical energy of a fuel

fuel standard In the United States, standards set for the fuel economy of cars, light trucks, and SUVs

geothermal power Power that comes from the intense heat within Earth

glacier A slow-moving mass or river of ice formed by compacted snow on high ground

global warming The gradual warming of Earth's surface and atmosphere as a result of carbon dioxide and other greenhouse gasses that trap heat

greenhouse effect The warming of Earth's surface by the natural effect of a blanket of certain gases in the atmosphere; the effect is increased by gases such as carbon dioxide produced by human activity, especially from burning fossil fuels

greenhouse gases Gases, such as carbon dioxide, that trap heat from the Sun within the atmosphere and help increase the greenhouse effect

habitat The natural environment in which a plant or animal lives

hydroelectric power Electrical power generated by moving water

ice age A period in history when large parts of Earth's surface were covered by ice sheets

nuclear power Power produced from nuclear reactions involving the splitting of atoms

oil sands Deposits that contain a heavy form of crude oil in solid or semi-solid form; also called tar sands

oil shale A rock that produces a substance similar to oil when it is heated using a special chemical process

photovoltaic cells Cells that collect sunlight and then convert it into electricity

pipeline A pipe or system of pipes, often located underground, designed to carry something such as oil or natural gas over a long distance

pollutant A harmful substance that damages or contaminates the air, soil, or water

protocol A formal agreement between nations

pumping rig The equipment used to pump oil and natural gas to the surface

radioactive waste Waste material from radioactive processes and facilities

ratify To give formal approval to something

recycling The process of using materials that have been used before to make new things

solar power Heat and light from the Sun harnessed as a form of renewable energy

summit A meeting between heads of government or their representatives to discuss important international matters

surface mine A mine in which the soil and rock overlying the mineral deposit are removed

turbine A machine powered by rotating blades; the motion generated can be transformed into electrical or mechanical power

United Nations (U.N.) An association of 192 states (as of 2008) that works to improve economic and social conditions and to solve political problems in a peaceful way

Further Information

Books

Graham, Ian. *Fossil Fuels: A Resource Our World Depends On* (Heinemann, 2004)

Morris, Neil. *Energy Sources: Fossil Fuels* (Smart Apple Media, 2007)

Snedden, Robert. *Essential Energy: Energy from Fossil Fuels* (Heinemann, 2006)

Stille, Darlene. *Natural Resources: Using and Protecting Earth's Supplies* (Compass Point Books, 2005)

Web sites

Alliance to Save Energy
www.ase.org
A non-profit organization committed to promoting energy efficiency worldwide. The ASE web site includes news and information about specific programs sponsored by the group, as well as tips on conserving energy.

International Energy Agency
www.iea.org
This international group focuses on ensuring reliable, affordable, and clean energy around the world. Its web site provides news, information, and statistics on different sources of energy, including fossil fuels, as well as the environment.

Union of Concerned Scientists
www.ucsusa.org/clean_energy
The Union of Concerned Scientists is an alliance of professionals who provide information about different types of energy, including fossil fuels, with facts about renewable energy, clean energy, and energy efficiency.

U.S. Department of Energy
www.fe.doe.gov
The U.S. DOE's Fossil Energy web site outlines its dedication to developing cleaner and more productive fossil fuel resources in the United States.

What Would You Do?

Page 7:
The advantages of coal are that it is still easy to obtain and it provides an inexpensive and reliable power source. A disadvantage is that coal supplies will eventually run out, so alternative fuel sources will be needed in the future. Also, coal-burning power plants produce air pollution, which causes health problems and contributes to global warming. Alternative energy sources include hydroelectric, solar, wind, nuclear power, and natural gas.

Page 15:
You could make the following points: opening certain areas to oil and natural gas exploration poses a threat to many different species that are already at risk because of the loss of ice in the Arctic regions. Invading their habitats with oil rigs and other equipment would put additional stress on them. Nations should find other energy sources that do not endanger animals and the environment.

Page 19:
You could state that nuclear power plants are safe and have had very few major accidents. Strict rules exist to protect plants from attack. The reactors are protected by steel-reinforced thick concrete, and the plants are surrounded by fences and guard towers. Governments are working to solve the problem of disposing of nuclear waste, such as burying it deep underground. In the meantime, most radioactive waste is safely stored.

Page 23:
Here are some points you can highlight: tell people that changing the way they get to work is good for them and the environment. If people do not drive, or if they carpool, they save money on gas. They can read or rest if they take public transportation. Walking or riding a bicycle is good for their health. Your ads can also suggest ways for companies to encourage their workers to carpool or use public transportation (companies can, for example, pay some of the commuting costs).

Page 31:
You could focus on the main effects of climate change: an increase in global temperatures (images of a heat wave, such as in Europe in 2007), a rise in sea levels and subsequent flooding (film of low-lying areas that are most prone to flooding, such as Bangladesh), a decrease in snow cover and melting of Arctic glaciers (Greenland and Antarctica), an increase in precipitation (a monsoon) and a greater frequency of drought (regions of Africa or Australia). You might also show nations that produce the most greenhouse gases, such as the United States and China.

Page 39:
Suggest that the government focus on developing an efficient public transportation system of trains and buses, preferably powered by alternative fuel sources. They should encourage people to take public transportation, ride bicycles, or carpool. The government can also offer lower taxes to manufacturers of cars that use alternative fuel sources. Laws could also ensure that all new vehicles are more fuel-efficient.

Page 45:
There are many things you can do. Lower the thermostat in the winter and raise it in the summer. Don't heat or cool your house when it's empty. Turn appliances off when they are not in use, and turn lights off when no one is in the room. Use compact fluorescent lightbulbs. Drive a fuel-efficient car. Whenever possible, walk, ride a bicycle, or take public transportation.

Index

Page numbers in **bold** refer to illustrations and charts.

About the Author
Jacqueline Laks Gorman has been a
writer and editor for more than 25 years.
Her books for young adults include
biographies and works in the social
sciences. She lives in DeKalb, Illinois,
with her husband and two children.